EARLY LEARN TO

SERIES

TALK TOGETHER BOOKS

The Lonely Giant

ANNE MURRAY-ROBERTSON
ROBERT ROBINSON

ILLUSTRATED BY MALCOLM LIVINGSTONE

A Piccolo Original
Piccolo Books

First published in 1987 by Pan Books Ltd,
Cavaye Place, London SW10 9PG

9 8 7 6 5 4 3 2 1

© Anne Murray-Robertson, Robert Robinson 1987

Illustrations by Malcolm Livingstone

ISBN 0 330 29854 2

Designed and typeset by
The Pen and Ink Book Co Ltd, London

Printed and Bound in Great Britain by
Springbourne Press Ltd, Basildon, Essex.

Produced by AMR for Pan Books Ltd

A note to parents

This book is designed for you and your child to enjoy
together. The early learning activities form a natural
part of the story, so read it aloud to your child and then
talk about the pictures together. Don't push the child to
answer the questions, but give plenty of help and
encouragement.

By following the adventures of Wizard Windrift and the
Lonely Giant, your child will practise the very important
skills of SORTING and MATCHING. In each picture
there are fun activities which will encourage your child
to match colours, shapes and patterns, as well as objects
to objects (eg. cup to saucer, needle to thread, and so
on). These activities will help your child with essential
skills necessary for early reading and early maths.

There are also a number of other useful activities which
you can do with your child in the home to reinforce
other early learning skills:

- sorting buttons for colour, shape or size
- matching shoes or socks for colours, patterns, size
- sorting the washing or ironing into piles for the
  family
- sorting the toys – soft, hard, new, old etc.
- sorting and matching crayons or pencils for colour
  and size

Longley the Giant looked like any other giant. He was just as big and strong, and looked every bit as fierce and frightening. But Longley was really a very different giant. Longley, you see, didn't like frightening people, and that was a problem. He was so big that everyone ran away from him.

Wizard Windrift was not afraid of Longley, but then Wizard Windrift was so magic that he was not afraid of anyone.
'Boo hoo,' sobbed Longley to the Wizard. 'I'm so lonely. I haven't got a friend.'

'Great snakeslegs,' said the Wizard, 'if you want a friend, we'll have to go and find one. We'll go through the door that has your picture on it. Which one is it?'

'But we're in your kitchen,' said Longley. 'Yes, and before we set out, you can tidy up for me,' replied the Wizard.

Can you find things which go together, and help Longley tidy up?

After they had tidied up, Wizard Windrift and Longley began their search for a friend. At last, they arrived at the gateway to Friendlyland.

They went through the gate into Friendlyland. 'Here are the Friendlyland wizards,' said Wizard Windrift. 'Find a hat for each wizard and they will help you.'

Because he had helped them find their hats, the wizards helped Longley. They gave him some magic shapes to open the magic door.

Longley looked at the door. 'Which shape will match the door lock?' he asked.

They passed through the magic door. 'Well done,' said Wizard Windrift. 'Here are some more Friendlyland people who need your help. Can you match the lost things to the people who lost them?'

Longley liked helping people. It was nice when they were not afraid of him any more. Then they came to the magic river.

Only one of the roads will take Longley over the river. Can you see which one it is?

Across the magic river, the half-witch was waiting for his help.

'Only half my spell has worked,' she said.

'Can you put us back together?'
Can you see which halves go together?

All the animals asked Longley if they could go with him to find new homes. 'Yes,' said Longley and smiled, and off they set.
'Now we must get through Spellbound Forest,' said Wizard Windrift. 'Can you say two words which sound like 'bat' to get us through?'
Can you think of two words?

Longley's words parted the trees and they found themselves in a clearing.
'Now find homes for my animal friends,' said Wizard Windrift.
Can you find a home for each of the Wizard's friends?

The end was in sight and Longley would soon find a friend. Wizard Windrift guided him to the gateway of Castle Friendly. 'You must find the key to open the gate.

I just hope you're not afraid of dragons,' said the Wizard.
Can you see the key?

It didn't take Longley long to find the key and open the gate. Inside was the Keeper of Friends.

'Help me to put these into pairs and I will help you,' the Keeper told Longley.

'Hooray,' cheered Wizard Windrift. 'You've earned a friend. Open this door and see who is there.' As soon as Longley opened the door, he knew he'd found a friend. 'I'm sure we'll like each other,' he said.
'I'm sure you're very much alike!' said Wizard Windrift.